JUL 0 2006

the Living Ocean

Tropical Oceans

Kelley MacAulay & Bobbie Kalman

🌳 Crabtree Publishing Company

www.crabtreebooks.com

Created by Bobbie Kalman

Dedicated by Kelley MacAulay
For Dylan Ramos, a beautiful and welcome addition to our family

Editor-in-Chief
Bobbie Kalman

Writing team
Kelley MacAulay
Bobbie Kalman

Substantive editor
Kathryn Smithyman

Editors
Molly Aloian
Robin Johnson
Rebecca Sjonger

Design
Margaret Amy Salter

Production coordinator
Heather Fitzpatrick

Photo research
Crystal Foxton

Consultant
Patricia Loesche, Ph.D., Animal Behavior Program,
Department of Psychology, University of Washington

Illustrations
Barbara Bedell: pages 14 (zooxanthellae), 20 (all except background),
    21 (moray eel and plankton)
Katherine Kantor: pages 20 (background), 21 (background)
Vanessa Parson-Robbs: page 21 (sea urchin and cardinal fish)
Bonna Rouse: page 17 (top)
Margaret Amy Salter: pages 14 (magnifing glass), 16, 17 (bottom),
    21 (magnifying glass, octopus, and sea grass)

Photographs
AP/Wide World Photos: page 28
Photograph courtesy of the Great Barrier Reef Marine Park Authority:
    page 31
SeaPics.com: Doug Perrine: pages 12, 13; Jeremy Stafford-Deitsch: page 23
© John Thompson: page 29
Other images by Corel, Digital Stock, Digital Vision, Photodisc,
    and Weatherstock

Crabtree Publishing Company

www.crabtreebooks.com   1-800-387-7650

Cataloging-in-Publication Data
MacAulay, Kelley.
  Tropical oceans / Kelley MacAulay & Bobbie Kalman.
    p. cm. -- (The living ocean series)
  ISBN-13: 978-0-7787-1300-5 (rlb)
  ISBN-10: 0-7787-1300-8 (rlb)
  ISBN-13: 978-0-7787-1322-7 (pbk)
  ISBN-10: 0-7787-1322-9 (pbk)
  1. Marine biology--Tropics--Juvenile literature. 2. Ocean--Tropics. I. Kalman, Bobbie.
II. Title. III. Series.
  QH95.59.M33 2006
  578.77'0913--dc22
                                                    2005019993
                                                        LC

**Published in
the United States**
PMB16A
350 Fifth Ave.
Suite 3308
New York, NY
10118

**Published
in Canada**
616 Welland Ave.,
St. Catharines, Ontario
Canada
L2M 5V6

**Published in the
United Kingdom**
73 Lime Walk
Headington
Oxford
OX3 7AD
United Kingdom

**Published
in Australia**
386 Mt. Alexander Rd.,
Ascot Vale (Melbourne)
VIC 3032

Contents

What are tropical oceans?

Oceans are large bodies of salt water. There are five oceans: Pacific, Atlantic, Indian, Arctic, and Southern. The oceans cover over three-quarters of the Earth's surface. **Tropical oceans** are the warm ocean waters that are found in the **tropics**. The tropics are hot regions of the Earth that are located near the **equator**, between the **Tropic of Cancer** and the **Tropic of Capricorn**. Tropical oceans are made up of the parts of the Pacific, Atlantic, and Indian oceans that are found in the tropics.

Deep, wide waters

The Pacific Ocean is the world's largest and deepest ocean. It covers almost 64 million square miles (166 million km²)! The average depth of the Pacific Ocean is 14,000 feet (4267 m). The second-largest ocean is the Atlantic Ocean. The Atlantic Ocean covers about 31 million square miles (80 million km²) and is about 11,000 feet (3353 m) deep in most places. The Indian Ocean is the third-largest ocean, covering about 28 million square miles (73 million km²). The average depth in the Indian Ocean is about 12,800 feet (3901 m).

Tropical lands

Many **continents** lie along the **coasts** of the tropical oceans. In fact, every continent except Antarctica touches tropical oceans in some place. The areas of land around the equator are covered mainly in tropical **rain forests**. The weather in rain forests is hot and humid for most of the year.

Rain forests receive rain nearly every day! The areas of land around the Tropic of Cancer and the Tropic of Capricorn are covered mainly in tropical **savannas**, or grasslands. Savannas are hot year round, but they have two different seasons: a long, dry winter and a short, wet summer.

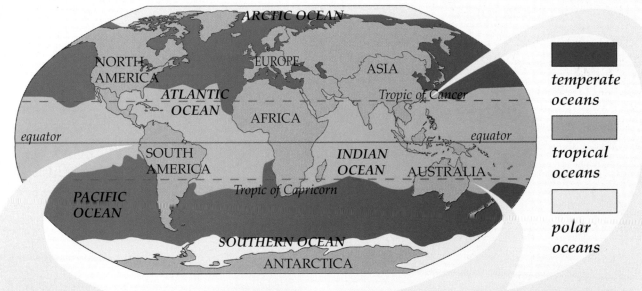

temperate oceans

tropical oceans

polar oceans

More than half of all the plants and animals on Earth live in tropical rain forests.

Tropical savannas have very few trees. Savanna animals live among bushes and grasses.

5

Clear, empty water

The year-round sunshine in the tropics causes the **surface**, or top, layers of tropical oceans to be warm and bright. The deep parts of tropical oceans remain cold and dark, however. The boundary between the warm surface waters and the cold, deep waters is called the **thermocline**. In tropical oceans, the **nutrients** that living things need are trapped beneath the thermocline, in the cold, deep waters.

Phytoplankton are microscopic green plants that need nutrients, especially **nitrogen** and **phosphorus**, to grow. Without these nutrients, few phytoplankton can grow in the surface layers of tropical oceans. Tropical oceans appear bright blue in color because they contain so little phytoplankton.

Without green plants, tropical ocean waters appear clear and bright blue.

Few living things

Since little phytoplankton grows in tropical oceans, very few animals can live in these waters. Phytoplankton are eaten by tiny animals, and these animals are then eaten by larger animals. This pattern of eating and being eaten is called a **food chain**. All ocean food chains depend on phytoplankton. Without it, there is not enough food in tropical oceans for many animals to eat.

It is hard for animals to find food in sunny tropical ocean waters.

Temperate mixing

Many plants and animals live in temperate oceans. Temperate oceans are found in places with changing seasons. In summer, these oceans have thermoclines because the sun heats up the top layers of the water. During winter, the thermoclines disappear because the surface layers of the water become cold. When both the surface and the deep parts of the oceans are cold, the deep, nutrient-rich waters mix with the waters at the surface. This mixing brings nutrients to the surface layers, allowing many plants and animals to live at the surface. Since tropical oceans are never cooled by cold winter weather, the nutrients remain trapped in the deep waters year-round.

Many plants grow in temperate oceans. The plants make temperate oceans appear dark blue or green.

Life in the great wide open

A few **species**, or types, of plants and animals live in the deep, **open** parts of tropical oceans. Many of these animals survive by using warm and cold ocean **currents** to find food. Currents are like rivers of water flowing through oceans.

Following warm currents

Warm currents flow from tropical oceans into temperate and polar oceans. Some tropical animals follow warm ocean currents from tropical waters into temperate waters, where there is more food. One such current is the **Gulf Stream**, which flows through the Atlantic Ocean from the Caribbean up the east coast of the United States. Warm currents move quickly—the Gulf Stream travels at about three to five miles per hour (4.8-8 kph). The Gulf Stream is much warmer than the waters surrounding it. In some places, warm ocean currents create **eddies**, or pockets of slow-moving warm waters. Tropical-ocean animals feed in the eddies for short periods of time.

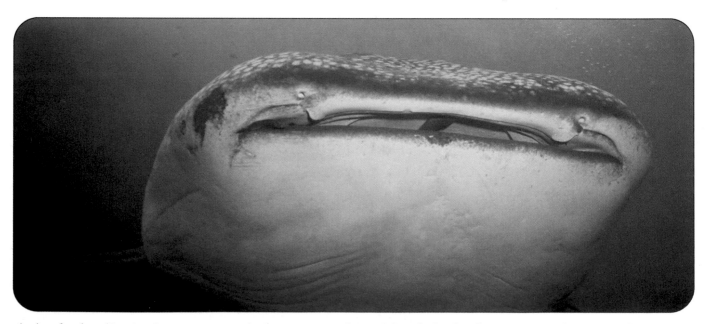

Animals that live in deep, open tropical waters, such as this whale shark, must travel constantly in search of food. The whale shark swims with its mouth open to take in tiny plants from the water.

Feeding in cold currents

Cold currents flow from polar and temperate oceans into tropical oceans. The **Humboldt Current**, which is also known as the Peru Current, is a cold current. Cold currents move slowly. The Humboldt Current moves at speeds of only one mile per hour (1.6 kph). It flows from the Southern Ocean into the Pacific Ocean, along the coasts of Chile and Peru.

Rich in nutrients

Cold currents are rich in nutrients, so many tropical ocean animals feed in these currents. Most tropical animals cannot survive for long in the cold temperatures of these currents, however. The animals stay near the edges of the currents, which are warmed by tropical waters.

Many kinds of whales and dolphins, including this pilot whale (top) and bottlenose dolphin (bottom), feed in the Humboldt Current.

Bustling communities

*A coral polyp's body is like a tube with a mouth on one end. The mouth is surrounded by stinging arms called **cnidae**. The polyp uses its cnidae to grab food.*

Scattered within tropical oceans are **coral reefs**, the richest **ecosystems** in the oceans. An ecosystem is a community of plants and animals and the area in which they live. Coral reefs are huge underwater structures that grow only close to coasts. For a coral reef to form, the waters must be about 70° F (21° C). Coral reefs are made up of **corals**. Corals are often mistaken for rocks or plants, but they are actually groups of tiny animals called **coral polyps**.

A polyp's body

There are two types of corals— **hard corals** and **soft corals**. Polyps that make up hard corals use a substance in ocean water called **calcium carbonate** to form hard, protective skeletons around their bodies. Polyps that make up soft corals do not form skeletons around their bodies. Only hard corals form coral reefs.

Hard corals, such as this brain coral, form coral reefs.

Adding layers

When coral polyps die, their skeletons are left behind. New polyps then grow on top of the skeletons. Over time, layer upon layer of skeletons build up. Eventually, they form the rocklike structure of a coral reef. Only the surface of the reef is made up of living coral polyps.

Types of coral reefs

Three types of coral reefs are found in tropical oceans—**fringing reefs**, **barrier reefs**, and **coral atolls**. All reefs begin as fringing reefs and change into barrier reefs over thousands of years. Barrier reefs eventually become coral atolls. The pictures on these pages show how corals reefs form and change over time.

Fringing reefs

Most coral reefs are fringing reefs. They grow along the coasts of newly formed tropical islands. An island forms when a volcano beneath the ocean erupts, and **lava** spills out onto the ocean floor. When the lava cools, it hardens. After many eruptions, the lava piles up until it rises above the surface of the water and forms an island. Over time, a fringing reef forms in the shallow waters around the island. Most of the corals on a fringing reef grow on the **reef front**, which is the side of the reef that faces the open ocean.

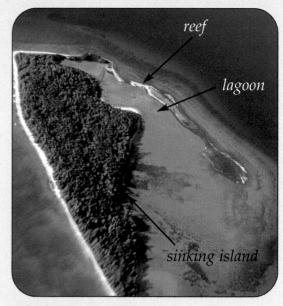

Barrier reefs

As the fringing reef grows, it adds a lot of weight to the island. Eventually, this added weight causes the island to begin sinking back into the ocean floor. As the island sinks, pools of water called **lagoons** form between the reef and the top of the sinking island. Once the lagoons form, the reef becomes a barrier reef.

Coral atolls

When the island sinks completely below the surface of the water, the reef becomes a coral atoll. A coral atoll has only a ring of land above the surface of the water. The reef has built up so much that the land rests on top of it. A coral atoll grows in a circular shape—the same shape as the reef that once surrounded the island. A large lagoon forms in the center of the circle.

land on top of reef

lagoon

The island is now below the surface of the water.

Volcanic islands

All islands in tropical oceans are either new volcanic islands or coral atolls, which are the remains of old volcanic islands. Volcanic islands are the tops of underwater volcanoes that have risen above the ocean's surface. Volcanic islands are **active**, **dormant**, or **extinct**. Active volcanic islands have erupted in the recent past. Dormant volcanic islands have not erupted for many years, but may erupt again. Extinct volcanic islands have not erupted for hundreds of years and are unlikely to erupt again. Most islands in tropical oceans are extinct volcanoes.

The world's largest active volcano, Mauna Loa, is on the tropical island of Hawaii. This enormous volcano covers over half the island! It last erupted in 1984.

Trading nutrients

Very little food is found in tropical oceans, except in coral reefs. To survive, many of the animals that live in coral reefs have **symbiotic relationships**. In symbiotic relationships, living things help one another survive. One of the most important symbiotic relationships is between coral polyps and **zooxanthellae**. Zooxanthellae are tiny plants that live inside the skin of coral polyps. The plants use nutrients from the waste of the polyps to perform **photosynthesis**. During photosynthesis, plants use the sun's energy to make their own food. As the zooxanthellae perform photosynthesis, they release nutrients back into the bodies of the coral polyps. By trading nutrients in this way, coral polyps and zooxanthellae help one another survive. Their survival makes it possible for a reef to grow. The reef itself then provides food and shelter for many other animals.

zooxanthellae

Working together

All the plants and animals in a coral reef are connected in a large symbiotic relationship. **Aquatic** plants need nitrogen and phosphorus to grow, but tropical oceans contain few of these nutrients. Nitrogen and phosphorus are present in the waters near the coral reef, however.

The many animals that live in and around the reef release nitrogen and phosphorus into the water through their waste. Aquatic plants use these nutrients to grow. The plants then provide food for fish to eat.

Many living things survive in coral reefs because nutrients are recycled between plants and animals.

Part-time residents

Some animals **migrate** from temperate oceans to tropical oceans. To migrate means to travel long distances to a new area for a certain period of time. In autumn, humpback whale mothers migrate to tropical waters to have their babies. Whales have their babies in tropical waters because very few animals that eat baby whales live in these waters.

Whale meals

Before the whale mothers migrate in autumn, they eat as much food as they can in the temperate waters. The whale mothers do not eat while they are in tropical waters. They live off the fat stored in their bodies. The baby whales drink their mothers' milk. In spring, the mother whales return to temperate waters with their babies.

Beach babies

Sea turtles are animals that leave their tropical ocean homes to lay eggs on beaches. Most sea turtles travel to beaches at night, when they are able to hide from predators. Sea turtle mothers crawl onto sandy beaches to **nest**, or dig nests and lay their eggs. They use their flippers to drag their bodies through the sand. When a turtle finds a wet spot on the beach, she uses her back flippers to dig a hole. She then lays a **clutch**, or group of eggs, in the nest. Depending on the species of sea turtle, the female lays between 50 and 150 eggs. After covering her eggs with sand, the mother turtle heads back to the ocean.

After laying a clutch of eggs, the sea turtle returns to the ocean. She leaves her eggs behind.

A race to the ocean

Sea turtle babies grow inside their eggs for 45 to 70 days. After hatching, the tiny babies dig their way out of the nest and begin crawling to the ocean. Many babies are eaten by predators, such as crabs and birds, as they crawl to the water. Once they are in the ocean, the babies swim away quickly. Some eventually reach coral reefs, where they live and find food.

Baby sea turtles are tiny, so their journey to the ocean is difficult and dangerous.

The Great Barrier Reef

The **Great Barrier Reef** is the world's largest coral reef. It stretches 1,429 miles (2300 km) off the northeastern coast of Australia. The Great Barrier Reef is actually made up of over 3,400 small coral reefs. It is home to thousands of different species of aquatic animals. Animals live in every nook and crack of the reef. The waters around the reef are filled with predators in search of food.

Hammerhead sharks are one of the largest shark species that live in the waters around the Great Barrier Reef.

The Great Barrier Reef is the largest structure on Earth made by living things.

Staying alive

The different animals that live in the Great Barrier Reef have different ways of avoiding predators. Some have **disruptive patterns**, such as stripes or spots, on their bodies. Disruptive patterns make it difficult for predators to tell where an animal's body begins or ends. Animals such as octopuses can change the colors of their bodies to blend in with the corals around them. Many brightly colored animals are poisonous. The bright colors act as a warning to predators. Some animals have small, thin bodies, which help them squeeze into cracks on the reef.

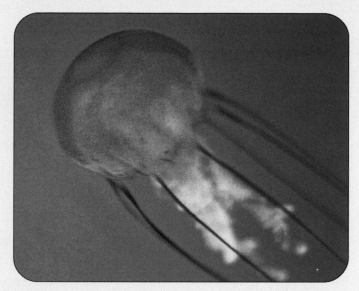

*Many sea jellies float in the sunlit waters around the Great Barrier Reef. Their bodies are **translucent**, or see-through. Predators find it difficult to see animals with translucent bodies.*

—an anemone's tentacle

*Anemones have stinging **tentacles** that keep away predators. Clown fish, however, have slimy coatings on their bodies that help them live safely among the stinging tentacles of anemones.*

Tropical ocean food webs

There are many food chains around the coral reefs in tropical oceans. A complete food chain is made up of a **carnivore**, a **herbivore**, and many plants. When an animal from one food chain eats plants or an animal from another food chain, the two food chains connect and form a **food web**. This page shows a daytime food web in the Great Barrier Reef. Page 21 shows a nighttime food web in the Great Barrier Reef. The arrows point toward the living things that are eating.

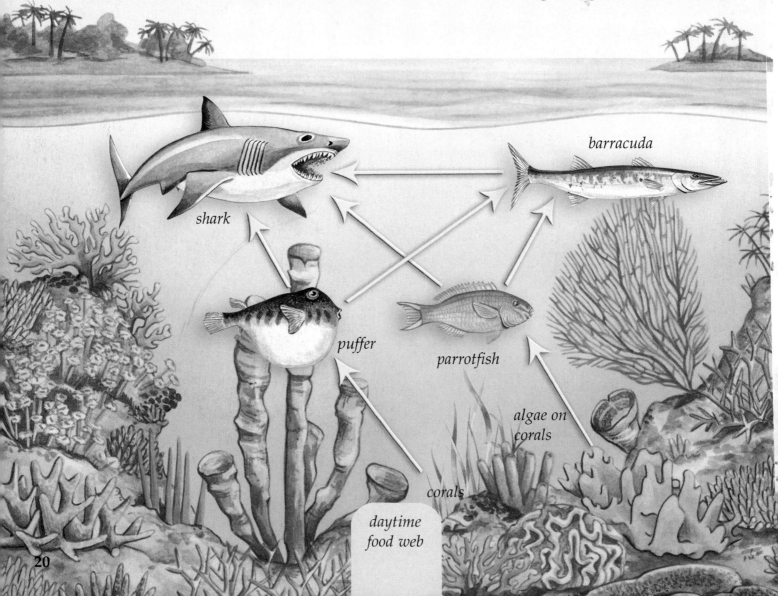

barracuda

shark

puffer

parrotfish

algae on corals

corals

daytime food web

Day and night

Coral reef food webs change from day to night because different animals are active at different times. Some animals are **diurnal**, whereas others are **nocturnal**. Diurnal animals hunt for food during the day. They are active in the daytime and rest at night by hiding in the reef. Nocturnal animals are active at night. They hunt at night and hide and rest during the day.

octopus

moray eel

plankton

tube sponge

scrawled fish

cardinal fish

sea urchin

sea grass

nighttime food web

Among the mangroves

Mangroves are trees that grow along or near the coasts of tropical oceans. They thrive in poor conditions that would kill most species of trees. For example, salt water kills most species of trees but mangroves can grow partially underneath salt water. Most trees grow only in soil that has plenty of **oxygen** in it, but mangroves grow in mud that has little oxygen. The roots of mangroves take in oxygen from the soil so that the trees can make their own food.

Root solutions

Some species of mangrove trees have **aerial roots**, or roots that grow above ground. Aerial roots are also known as **breathing roots**. By growing above ground, breathing roots take in oxygen from the air. Some mangrove species also have roots with **membranes** that **filter**, or remove, salt from the water as they take water into the roots. Other species take in water and salt, but they release the salt through their leaves.

Protecting the coasts

Mangroves are important parts of tropical ocean coasts. Mangrove roots help prevent **erosion**. Erosion is the washing away of land. Erosion causes coasts to be washed into oceans by **tides**. The thick tangles of mangrove roots surround coastal mud and keep it from being washed into the ocean. In addition to protecting the soil, mangrove roots provide homes for many tropical plants and animals. Fish often use the sheltered mud around mangrove roots as **nurseries** for their babies. A nursery is a place where young fish can grow safely.

Plenty to eat

Mangrove trees also provide important sources of food for many animals. As mangrove leaves die, they fall into the water around the trees and add nutrients to the water. These added nutrients attract many kinds of fish, crabs, worms, and sea jellies to the area. Animals such as egrets, white ibises, banded finches, and herons also live among the branches of mangrove trees.

Many animals find food and shelter among the tangle of underwater mangrove roots.

23

Swirling storms

eye

Violent storms called **hurricanes** often form over tropical oceans. Hurricanes are huge storms that can be hundreds of miles across. They often travel at speeds of 15 to 20 miles per hour (24-32 kph). The ocean waters in which hurricanes form must be 80° F (27° C) or warmer to a depth of 150 feet (46 m), so hurricanes form only over tropical oceans. Hurricanes last for a week or longer because they get stronger from the warm ocean waters over which they form.

How it begins

Hurricanes begin as thunderstorms that have winds of about 38 miles per hour (61 kph). As the winds get stronger, they begin to move in a **cyclonic**, or swirling, pattern. The winds move around a center point of the storm, called an **eye**. Although the storm's force is often greatest near the eye, conditions inside the eye itself are calm. The eye of a hurricane is usually between 20 to 40 miles (32-64 km) across.

Heading for land

Some hurricanes blow over islands and onto the coasts of continents. Hurricanes **dissipate**, or lose energy, quickly over land, without the warm ocean waters that feed them. In a short time, however, hurricanes can destroy towns and cities near coasts. Strong winds topple buildings and trees.

Storm surges cause flooding and damage beaches. A storm surge is a large amount of ocean water that is sucked up into the eye as a hurricane nears land. When the storm reaches land, the water is released. Each year, hurricanes cause millions of dollars in damage to tropical lands and take the lives of hundreds of people.

Hurricane Katrina

On August 29, 2005, Hurricane Katrina, one of the most powerful hurricanes in American history, struck the **Gulf Coast**, devastating cities in Louisiana, Mississippi, and Alabama. When the hurricane hit the coast, it had winds of 125 miles per hour (201 kph) and it was carrying a huge storm surge. The strength of the winds destroyed parts of the **levees** that surround New Orleans, Louisiana. Levees are walls that are built to keep surrounding waters out of cities. When the levees broke, water from the storm surge poured into New Orleans, flooding almost the entire city. Thousands of people who had been unable to **evacuate**, or leave the area, were stranded for days without food or water. In all four states, hundreds of people were killed by the storm, and thousands of people were left without homes, businesses, or schools.

broken levee

This image shows water flooding into New Orleans because of a broken levee.

25

The effects of El Niño

Forest fires caused by El Niño destroy homes and property. They also kill many animals and destroy the places where animals live.

As flood waters rise, people must move from their homes to higher ground. When they return, they often find that the flood waters have destroyed their homes.

El Niño is the unusual warming of surface waters in the tropical areas of the Pacific Ocean. It occurs off the coasts of Peru and Ecuador. The rise in water temperatures is caused when **trade winds** change direction. Trade winds are winds that blow toward the equator from the northeast in the **Northern Hemisphere** and from the southeast in the **Southern Hemisphere**.

Wrong-way winds

Normally, trade winds blow tropical waters from east to west across the Pacific Ocean in December. These winds carry warm waters away from South America toward Australia and Indonesia. About every seven years, however, the trade winds change direction, and El Niño occurs. During El Niño, the warm waters are pushed toward South America. Warm ocean waters **evaporate**, or change into vapor, and then form clouds, which blow over lands and cause rain. The extra rain causes flooding in South America. Without the warm waters, Australia and Indonesia do not receive enough rain. As a result, these areas experience **droughts** and forest fires.

El Niño also affects weather patterns around the world. In North America, Canada often has warmer winters during El Niño years, whereas the United States has much colder winters. The cold weather in the United States can destroy entire seasons of crops, such as the ice-covered citrus plant shown above.

Broken food chains

Most years, the waters along the coasts of South America become colder in December, as the warm waters are blown westward. The colder waters reduce the thermocline, allowing the nutrient-rich deep waters to rise to the surface and add phytoplankton to it. The phytoplankton are eaten by many plant-eating animals, and the plant-eating animals feed many carnivores. This pattern is broken during El Niño years. The nutrient-poor warm waters brought by the trade winds block the nutrient-rich deep waters from rising to the surface. As a result, phytoplankton cannot grow during El Niño, and many animals starve.

In 1998, the effects of El Niño caused most of the anchovies on Peru's coast to die. Anchovies are the main source of food for sea lions. Without their main food source, thousands of sea lions starved to death that year.

Terrible tsunamis!

A **tsunami** is a series of waves caused by an **earthquake** or a volcanic eruption on the ocean floor. When an earthquake or eruption occurs, a huge amount of water is **displaced**, or forced out of its normal position. The displaced water forms waves that rush away from the area where the disturbance took place. The waves can be over 60 miles (97 km) long and travel at speeds of up to 450 miles per hour (724 kph). The waves are harmless in the deep ocean, however, because they are usually less than a foot (30 cm) high.

Walls of water

As the waves of a tsunami approach a coast, they slow down and begin to grow in height. By the time the tsunami reaches land, the waves may be over 100 feet (30 m) tall in some places. These powerful waves rush onto land, knocking over everything in their paths. Further damage to property and the environment occurs when floating **debris** crashes into buildings and trees.

The image above shows a huge tsunami wave crashing onto land.

The Tsunami Disaster

On December 26, 2004, a massive earthquake beneath the Indian Ocean created one of the most destructive tsunamis in history. This event has become known as "The Tsunami Disaster." The earthquake that created the tsunami was so powerful, that it caused the entire Earth to shudder. Huge amounts of water were displaced, creating a tsunami with waves as high as 50 feet (15 m) in some places. The waves slammed into eleven countries surrounding the Indian Ocean. Countries near the area where the earthquake took place, such as Indonesia, were struck by the tsunami within minutes of the earthquake. Countries farther away from the location of the earthquake, such as Sri Lanka and India, were hit hours later. The tsunami even traveled over 3,000 miles (4828 km) across the ocean to Africa, where more people lost their lives. Over 200,000 people were killed in the disaster, and thousands of others were left without homes, food, or clean drinking water. Countries from around the world sent aid workers and supplies into the devastated countries. They also donated millions of dollars to help people rebuild their communities and homes.

This picture shows an area along a beach in Indonesia before the tsunami occured.

This picture shows the same area after the December 2004 Tsunami Disaster.

Tropical oceans in trouble

The careless actions of people put tropical oceans in danger. When people throw garbage on beaches, the garbage eventually washes into oceans. The tides carry the garbage along the coasts and far into the open ocean. Some ocean animals die when they eat garbage that they mistake for food. Other animals are killed when they become tangled in garbage and cannot swim. When the tides cause garbage to smash into coral reefs, it damages the reefs or causes parts of the reefs to break off. When the reefs are destroyed, many tropical ocean animals lose their homes and the areas in which they find food.

Fishing for trouble

People also damage tropical oceans by **overfishing**. To overfish is to take too many of one species of animal from a certain area. When people overfish a species, they threaten its population in that area of the ocean and also leave predators in the area with less food.

Some divers do not know how fragile coral reefs are. Divers permanently damage coral reefs if they touch them in any way. Even careful divers may kick off parts of the reefs accidentally with their feet.

People can help!

Many people recognize that tropical oceans are important ecosystems that need protection. One way people are working to protect tropical oceans is by creating **marine parks**. Marine parks are areas of oceans that are protected by governments. A government can stop people from polluting these areas and also restrict harmful activities such as fishing and boating.

Protecting the reef

Most of the Great Barrier Reef is a protected marine park called the Great Barrier Reef Marine Park. The park is managed by a government group called the Great Barrier Reef Marine Park Authority. This group enforces rules that protect the reef and the animals that live there. It allows people to do some fishing around the reef, but they control carefully how many fish are taken. The group also makes sure that the places where fishing occurs are spread across a large area, so that no area is overfished. The marine park authority monitors tourism on the reef, as well. It instructs tourists not to touch the reef or remove animals or corals from it. By educating tourists, the marine park authority helps people enjoy the reef without harming it.

This member of the Great Barrier Reef Marine Park Authority is examining part of the reef to make sure it has not been damaged by tourists or pollution.

Glossary

Note: Boldfaced words that are defined in the text may not appear in the glossary.

aquatic Describing a living thing that grows or lives in water

carnivore An animal that eats other animals

coast The land at the edge of an ocean

continent One of the seven main areas of land on Earth—Asia, Africa, North America, South America, Europe, Australia, and Antarctica

debris The remains of objects that have been broken or destroyed

drought A long period of time when little or no rain falls

earthquake A violent shaking of the ground, often causing destruction

Gulf Coast A region of the United States that borders the Gulf of Mexico

herbivore An animal that eats mainly plants

lava Hot liquid rock that travels from deep in the Earth to the Earth's surface

membrane A thin layer of skin

nitrogen A colorless, odorless gas found in air and water that all living things need to stay healthy

Northern Hemisphere The half of the Earth that stretches from the equator to the North Pole

nutrients Substances that are needed by living things to stay healthy

open Describing ocean waters that are far from shore

oxygen A gas that is part of air and water, which animals and people need to breathe

phosphorus A chemical that all living things need to stay alive

polar oceans The Arctic Ocean and the Southern Ocean—cold oceans located at the Earth's poles

rain forest A forest that receives over 80 inches (203 cm) of rain each year

Southern Hemisphere The half of the Earth that stretches from the equator to the South Pole

temperate oceans Parts of oceans that are located in areas where the seasons change

tides The rise and fall of water levels along coasts

Index

1 2 3 4 5 6 7 8 9 0 Printed in the U.S.A. 4 3 2 1 0 9 8 7 6 5